Elizabeth Austen

D0898672

✳ Smithsonian

Consultants

Brian Mandell
Program Specialist
Smithsonian Science Education Center

Chrissy Johnson, M.Ed.
Teacher, Cedar Point Elementary
Prince William County Schools, Virginia

Sara Cooper, M.Ed.
Third Grade Teacher
Fullerton School District

Publishing Credits

Rachelle Cracchiolo, M.S.Ed., *Publisher*
Conni Medina, M.A.Ed., *Editor in Chief*
Diana Kenney, M.A.Ed., NBCT, *Series Developer*
Emily R. Smith, M.A.Ed., *Content Director*
Véronique Bos, *Creative Director*
Robin Erickson, *Art Director*
Michelle Jovin, M.A., *Associate Editor*
Mindy Duits, *Series Designer*
Lee Aucoin, *Senior Graphic Designer*
Smithsonian Science Education Center

Image Credits: p.17 Auscape/UIG via Getty Images; all other images from iStock and/or Shutterstock.

Library of Congress Cataloging-in-Publication Data

Names: Rice, Dona, author. | Smithsonian Institution.
Title: Staying warm / Dona Herweck Rice.
Description: Huntington Beach, CA : Teacher Created Materials, [2020] | "Smithsonian." | Audience: K to grade 3. |
Identifiers: LCCN 2018049785 (print) | LCCN 2018054693 (ebook) | ISBN 9781493868919 (eBook) | ISBN 9781493866519 (pbk.)
Subjects: LCSH: Body temperature--Regulation--Juvenile literature. | Dwellings--Heating and ventilation--Juvenile literature. | Heating--Juvenile literature. | Cold--Juvenile literature.
Classification: LCC QP135 (ebook) | LCC QP135 .R4557 2020 (print) | DDC 612/.01426--dc23
LC record available at https://lccn.loc.gov/2018049785

Teacher Created Materials

5301 Oceanus Drive
Huntington Beach, CA 92649-1030
www.tcmpub.com

ISBN 978-1-4938-6651-9

Table of Contents

Too Cold

The air is cold. Your skin has tiny **goose bumps**. It is time to warm up!

This person's arm has goose bumps.

Warming Up

When it is cold, people may want to warm up. There are many ways to do it.

Blowing warm air on your hands may warm them up.

Shaking and Shivering

People may **shiver** when they are cold. Shivering happens when muscles twitch. They twitch to make heat.

Cover Up

People's bodies make heat. Clothes and blankets help bodies keep their heat. Good **shelter** does too.

A thick sweater helps keep in body heat.

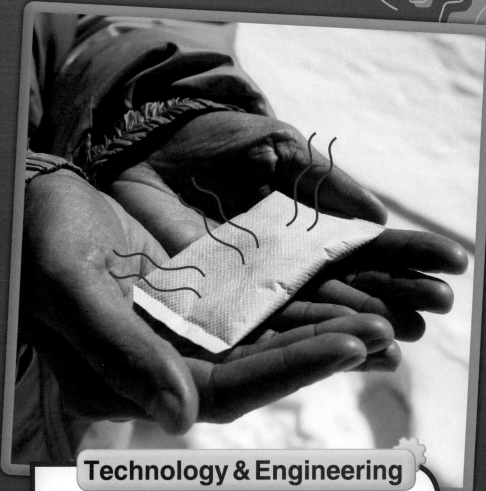

Hand Warmers

A reaction happens inside hand warmers. The reaction gives off heat. Warm hands help the whole body feel warm.

Fire Up

Fires help people stay warm. They can heat anything near them. Just be careful!

They read in front of a warm fire.

A group of friends stays warm by a campfire.

Heat Up

People use heaters to stay warm. They heat homes and buildings. They keep people warm on cold days.

These heaters can be used to heat homes.

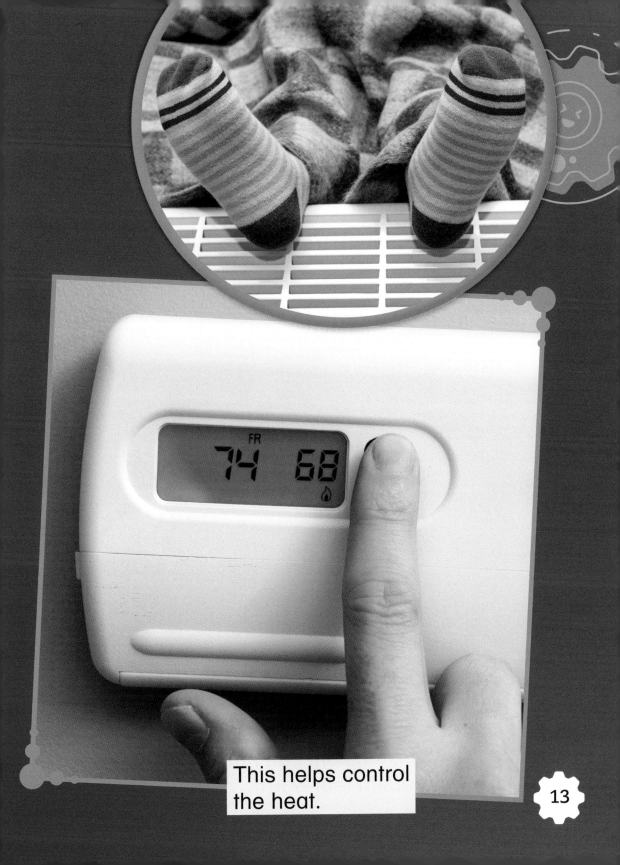

This helps control
the heat.

Drink Up

A warm drink can make a person feel warm inside. It can also be a nice treat on a cold day.

Hot chocolate can make a person feel warm.

This girl eats warm soup.

Perk Up

People can get warm at any time. Just start moving! Their bodies warm up right away.

This boy stays warm by moving around.

Penguin Huddles

Penguins **huddle** up to stay warm. They stand in the best shape and pattern to keep all the penguins warm.

Hot Stuff

Everyone needs warmth. It is a good thing there are so many ways to warm up!

These friends dress warmly on a cold day.

This girl stays warm with a blanket.

STEAM CHALLENGE

The Problem

Your class is on a field trip far from shelter. All of a sudden, the weather gets very cold. You need shelter to stay warm. There are trees all around you. You have blankets. But there are not enough for everyone. What do you do?

The Goals

- Design a model of a shelter about the size of a sheet of paper.
- Design a model with sticks, clay, leaves, yarn, and/or fabric.
- Design an entrance to the shelter that is big enough to fit your hand through.

1 Research and Brainstorm

Why do people need to stay warm? How does shelter help keep people warm?

2 Design and Build

Draw your plan. How will it work? What materials will you use? Build your model!

3 Test and Improve

Place your hand inside your shelter. Place a bowl of ice outside your shelter. Blow on the ice toward your shelter. Can you feel the cold air? Can you make it better? Try again.

4 Reflect and Share

Why is it important for the whole class to be in the shelter? What else could the class do to get and stay warm?

Glossary

goose bumps

huddle

shelter

shiver

Career Advice
from Smithsonian

Do you want to design ways to keep people warm? Here are some tips to get you started.

"Read how people have stayed warm over the years. Then, try making your own tools and gear to stay warm." *— Tim Winkle, Curator*

"Study science and engineering. You should also learn about animals and plants, such as sheep and cotton. And reading about art will teach you about design." *— Madelyn Shaw, Curator*